THE STREET

POEMS AND BALLADS

of

JOHN B. KEANE

Selected and edited
by
JOANNA KEANE O'FLYNN

MERCIER PRESS

MERCIER PRESS
Douglas Village, Cork
www.mercierpress.ie

Trade enquiries to COLUMBA MERCIER DISTRIBUTION,
55a Spruce Avenue, Stillorgan Industrial Park, Blackrock, Dublin

ISBN: 1 85635 415 6

10 9 8 7 6 5 4 3 2 1

Some of the material in this book originally appeared in *The Street and other poems* in 1961 and was published by Progress House (Publications) Ltd. of 36 Home Farm Road, Dublin 9.

DEDICATION
To the Keane and O'Flynn grandchildren
so adored by John B.

The publishers gratefully acknowledge the financial assistance of the Arts Council/An Chomhairle Ealaíon

Printed in Ireland by Colour Books Ltd.

John B. Keane's Kerry Blessing

That the frost may never afflict your spuds,
That your cabbages may always be free from worms,
That the crows might never pick your stack,
That your she-goat might never dread the puck,
And should you by good fortune, come into
the possession of a female donkey,
May she be in foal.

Calefacted by the monks of Ballybunion who
eventually succumbed to their own produce.

Contents

Foreword

'No mun, no, fun, your son', my father, still in his teens, wrote in desperation to his own father, William Keane, while on a camping adventure with his friends in Ballybunion.

'How sad, too bad, your dad', my grandfather quipped back.

Up to his death last year, John B. spoke in verse and song in his everyday exchanges with family and friends. 'O Jimmy Boylan, you are always smiling', he would sing to a Cork companion of the same name. His language was naturally alliterative, assonantal, magical and musical.

'He was a poet before anything else', my mother remarked of late concerning John B. Indeed included in this revised anthology are 'Wagtail' and 'The Street' composed when my father was only seventeen. The then president of St Michael's College reprimanded him for these first forays into poetry disbelieving that they could be his own work. Ironically, this cynicism served only to drive him to experiment further with his craft.

Throughout their happy lives, my parents were engaged in a love affair punctuated by passion, deep love and unflinching devotion to each other. 'Two Eyes' was published in *The Kerryman* newspaper in March 1950 in dedication to my mother. 'Two Lips', a sister poem, from my mother's private collection of poems is also included in this anthology. During their courtship, in the early 1950s, he wrote letters and poems unrelentingly to her in an impeccable hand – from Listowel and later England to her native Ahaneboy, Knocknagoshel – always affectionately addressing her as Mague. 'Two Lips', 'Tryst', 'Yesterday' and 'Delight' are all published for the first time in this collection.

My father was deeply proud of his native Listowel. In the latter stages of his life, he could not bear to be away from his beloved town for more than three days. Privately, and in public interviews, he unceasingly paid tribute to the town that bore and shaped him. He eagerly engaged with the vitality and vibrancy of his colourful town. He speaks lyrically and touchingly about the River Feale, most notably in 'Feale Waters'. One of his last compositions, the song 'Sweet Listowel', was written as a promise to a neighbour, bookie Eric Browne. Whether inebriated or cold sober, John B. could burst into song at any given moment.

Last year, John B. spoke to some of my students on the art of writing. 'I'd love him for a dad', one girl remarked afterwards. He was optimistically approaching his seventy-fourth birthday when he gently slipped away from us on a bright May morning. John B. wrote about his own father, also seventy-three when he passed away:

> I am terribly proud of my father,
> Bitterly, faithfully proud.
> Let none say a word to my father
> Or mention his name out loud.

The same words ring true about his son.

JOANNA KEANE O'FLYNN

May 2003

Introduction

Poems of a Man who Loved Love

John B. Keane wrote poems at different times in his life. As a young man, he wrote quite a lot, but as he turned his attention more and more to plays, his poetic output understandably diminished. Yet he always kept in touch and this new collection has all the imaginative vitality and variety, the linguistic energy, the blend of humour and compassion, the sharp powers of observation, the love of nature, the understanding of people, the love of music, the lifelong appreciation of drink and drinking companions, and that tolerant open-mindedness towards different kinds of experience that characterises all his work. Readers of this book, these poems, ballads and songs, will be struck, once again, by the warm humanity of the man who wrote them, and by the scrupulous, traditional skills with which he expressed that humanity.

Songs. Music. Ballads. Football. Love. Sex. Emigration. Fulfilment. Disappointment. Time. Marriage. Dublin. London. Listowel. Always lovely Listowel. And the River Feale. John B.'s beloved Mary, her beauty and kindness. His love of freedom. His dislike of all forms of tyranny, including spiritual fascism. His father, 'a lovely man', 'a loveable man'. His ability to appreciate the lives of both country people and people of the town. His ability to face the problems of loneliness and his robust savouring of the delights of pleasure. The beautiful, moving, cutting songs from his plays. The poet in the dramatist. The dramatist in the poet. And always, the passionate sense that here is a writer with a deep love of life in all its complexity. From beginning to end, John B. Keane was a lover. It was this love that drove him on. Love of language. Love of poetry and music. Love of Mary and his family. Love of justice. Love of people. Love of love.

He could be satirical too. There are poems here that show his caustic side. Caustic, but not bitter. The lover wins through in the end.

I'll end by quoting a couple of verses from one of my favourite poems by that great and gallant soul. The poem is entitled 'Leaving Home for the First Time'.

All over Feale river the shadows are falling.
And deep in Shanowen the vixen is calling.
The sweet night is young, love; the night is forever.
And shadows are falling all over Feale river.

Oh, my love, my first love, the salmon are leaping.
Lie still, my hard heart, my beloved is sleeping.
The sweet night is young, love; tonight is forever.
The shadows are falling all over Feale river.

BRENDAN KENNELLY

The Street

I love the flags that pave the walk.
I love the mud between,
The funny figures drawn in chalk.
I love to hear the sound
Of drays upon their round,
Of horses and their clock-like walk.
I love to watch the corner-people gawk
And hear what underlies their idle talk.

I love to hear the music of the rain.
I love to hear the sound
Of yellow waters flushing in the main.
I love the breaks between
When little boys begin
To sail their paper galleons in the drain.
Grey clouds sail west and silver-tips remain.
The street, thank God, is bright and clean again.

Here, within a single little street,
Is everything that is,
Of pomp and blessed poverty made sweet
And all that is of love
Of man and God above.
Of happiness and sorrow and conceit,
Of tragedy and death and bitter-sweet,
Of hope, despair, illusion and defeat.

A golden mellow peace forever clings
Along the little street.

There are so very many lasting things
Beyond the wall of strife
In our beleaguered life.
There are so many lovely songs to sing
Of God and His eternal love that rings
Of simple people and of simple things.

John B. was born in Church Street, Listowel on 21 July 1928. He wrote
this poem in his late teens about his beloved birthplace. Awash with
boarding houses, 'eating houses', harness-makers, public houses, a thri-
ving drapery, a millinery shop and assorted businesses, this street and
its warm comfortable characters fascinated and enchanted the aspiring
poet.

    Incidentally, the closing lines of this poem are engraved on his grave.

The Wagtail

I

On wings of ebony the morning crow has drifted,
School-time.
Remembering a wagtail I hurry
To inevitable doom.
A crude theatrical teacher
Fills me with worry.
But I remember the wagtail
Dipping his tail in shallow water.

II

To the pulsing classroom arrives old torment
Hates me
I am in cap and bell's dispensary.
No tears nor yielding now.
Am wholly indestructible
Quite soon without hurry
I shall visit my friend Bill Wagtail
Dipping slim wings in shallow water.

An Ardent True-Lover

He is the same as us, they said,
He is the same as us.
He angers and makes a fuss, they said,
He is the same as us.

They were wrong for I behaved
As a child or as a monkey mimics.
I raved the moment they raved
And suited myself to their gimmicks.

'He is the same as us,' they said,
'Battens on drink and quarrels.'
'Oh, he is the same as us,' they said,
'See how he ogles the girls.'

'And she followed, a woman in red', they said,
'She has not loved before.'
'He is the same as us,' they said,
But they weren't so sure any more.

'His nose and his mouth and his head shall be bled.
We will razor his groin without suture.
We will never be sure again,' they said;
'We will never be sure in the future.'

But I will be gone while they're counting the sands;
I will move like a 'bolt when they're moving.
And I will be hunting in different lands
And loving while they are reproving.

The Trapped Ones

I

I would go down amid the dunes
At first giddy flow of tide
And engage the sperm-peopled waters
Giddily twirling long liquid moustachios.
When pools are brimful
I would tread caressing fronds
And snare the fulsome sea-fish.
Sweet sizzling of delicious flesh
Should beckon you from sleep.

II

Or with bright shafts of dawn
Through wild mountain meadows stride
Plucking the pink-bellied mushroom
From dewy bosoms of green grassiness,
Pluck wild florets tinted
To virgin colouring, with defilade
Of dripping clover round them.
These upon your pillow resting
Should lure you out of sleep.

III

No! – we would marry and decline
In some three-roomed Gethsemane
And your feet that should be all artistry

Would swell to shapeless trunks of fleshiness
From bearing of children.
I would tire of the unending labour.
I would weary of the anaemic face,
The ill-groomed hair, the sickliness
Of things without sunshine.

Protracting an Affair of Love

Perhaps you might remember an interlude
Or sad occasion that appealed to you.
An old man's humours, a father's rectitude,
Or girlish confidence that was revealed to you.

Murmur, so that your lips will intimate
More loving. There is no satiety.
I need to affirm bond my sweet associate.
Latterly there will be ample time for piety,

Something whatsoever to protract our lying.
The lighting of another cigarette.
Soon the grey-haired harbingers of dying
Will rust our hearts with age and thought of death.

Letter to Jack McIntyre, Esquire

If undelivered, return to
Katherine Margaret McHugh,
Cat's Lane, Park View,
London, NW2.

My dear Jack,
You will be pleased to hear
I am willing to marry you, my dear.
This time back I have been wild
As to the father of my child.
I tried the places he used to stay
Only to find he'd gone away.
I heard in a city kip
That he was now married to a rip
Like himself in the north somewhere.
That's a thought I cannot bear
Thinking of him in a bed
With some other strap instead.
Oh, Jack I love him still
And I suppose I always will.
It was good of you to inquire
If I would be a McIntyre.
Well, Jack, you know I love him
And with this worry I have grown slim,
But since I have a good figure, too,
I might be of some use to you.
When I look back and think
Of the way he used to drink
And how he fooled me so much

While there was never such
A fine gentleman as you.
When we were courting you were always true.
I was a fool to leave you down.
My mother said I was an awful clown.
You were so steady, like, and sound –
I mean, you knew the value of a pound
And still you always stood your round;
He was mean and very small.
He was really a horrible thing
And the smutty songs he used to sing
And then the way he disappeared
When the thing happened that we feared.
Well, Jack, that's about all I have to say
Except, I'll be waiting for you every day.
I'm so happy now, Jack, I could sing;
And, Jack, don't forget an engagement ring.
You could get a marriage one for ten and six.
They're very cheap. Bye. Love. X, X; X, X, X.

Letter to Katherine Margaret McHugh

Same place, London W2.
From the said Jack McIntyre,
Esquire.

My dearest Kate,
It was all hours late
When I finished milking last night.
Your letter gave me an awful fright
Until I read it and then I knew
You meant me to be a husband to you.
I'll be over on the next boat –
Pray to God 'twill stay afloat.
Of course I'll buy the engagement ring
And on top of that, I'll bring
Enough money for a honeymoon.
I have dry cattle now in Glounsharoon
And twelve milking in the home place.
What a terrible disgrace
That other fellow turned out to be.
I'm glad you think he's not like me.
You won't have to milk or wash or scrub.
We'll get a serving girl to do every job.
I'm on my way to the boat, my love.
I'll see you in two days, with God's help above.

Last Letter of Katherine Margaret McHugh

To Jack McIntyre, so true

Oh, my poor dear foolish Jack;
Too late now to tell you turn back
Jack, I've great news today!
I've heard from him: he's not far away.
This morning I got his call,
And, Jack, he's not married at all,
So when you come, I won't be here,
I'll be gone to him, the poor dear.
Don't be too disappointed, Jack,
And don't be in too much of a hurry back.
There's a good cowboy on at the Palace
About a sheriff in a place, I think, called Dallas.
You used to like cowboys, and sex.
Goodbye, Jack. X, X; X, X, X.

Feale Waters

When you have gone away
To leave me with the quiet night,
And with the long empty day.
Then I shall learn to love you once again,
My darling, as I loved you long ago
Between the quiet hours we knew in our glen
Beside the willows where Feale waters flow.

And I shall dream how one time when the bird
Had sung his heart's companion to her rest
When no sound save the falling down of night was heard,
I dared to lay my hand upon your full, white breast.

You turned your eyes upon me, and your lips
Were moist and sweet, my long lost treasure trove
Like silken petal blooms your fingertips
Soothed my tired eyes and strummed the sweet chords of
    love.

The Feale river is Listowel's principal river. Popular for salmon and sea trout fishing, the Feale both inspired and stimulated John B. and Bryan McMahon in poetry and song. Rising in North Cork, this celebrated river braves an arduous journey as it adventures through hills, bogland and valleys, passing through Abbeyfeale in Co. Limerick and on to Listowel until it eventually meets the sea in Ballybunion.

Nothing Matters

The heart empties utterly
The breast aches and pains
There is nothing, nothing whatever,
All is emptiness.

The mind pursues the spiritual
Spirit is less than a mote
Nothing matters, all is perplexity,
Pitiful, human.

Others, millions and millions,
Unborn, living dead.
Quickly hold hands; diminish
Endless emptiness.

But quickly now, clarity
Man woman and child
Stand fast, hearts unity
In last loveliness!

Unity, strive to nullify
The misinterpreted creed
Of Christ's condemnation
Since He loves us.

How Ignorant Men are Misled by Ignorance

I knew a maker of nets,
A common, ungainly man.
He would order a pair of wets,
And then he would order again.

I was forced into his company,
I am somewhat ashamed to admit;
But, tell me, who can foresee
Life, or the meaning of it?

But that is a different story –
Forgive me if I digress –
You have your particular worry,
And I have mine, too, I confess.

This maker of nets was a fool.
There are things one can never forget
Went half through a primary school.
In addition he bored me to death.

I do not work with my hands.
There is no job to my taste.
Digging indelicate lands
To me seems nonsensical waste.

'You have the trade of a bum!' he said.
'A delicate trade,' said he.
'My nails are black and my hand so red
That no one considers me.'

'Here is a piece of string.
Here at this side is the end;
And here is the beginning.
Now which is which, my friend?'

I said: 'This side is the end.'
'No!' he said, 'the beginning.
The other side is the end.'
He said: 'Try it again since I'm winning.'

I tried it again but each time
He laughed and he said 'My friend,
I admire your immediate claim.
But the other side is the end.'

I might have profited suddenly
If he would only relinquish
The secret soul of his art or if I
Had the sight of my eyes to distinguish.

He said, 'here is a piece of string
Here at this end is the end
And here is the beginning
Now which is which my friend?'

Certainty

This is the place, I was told.
See the tall grass lie low.
They rested here and made bold.
Now for a certainty I know.

Take note of the blue-bell broken,
The fern mangled and dead,
And look at this for a token –
Here's a hair from her head!

Late Night Review

Now that many nights of similarity have passed
And day upon day of gradual surcease
And some maturity has sown its doubtful seed
I am somewhat of a man in principle at last,
Compelled to manhood by varied imperfections,
And mellowed with dreaming of a lost pale girl.

Time now to review the fretful summary
Of some kind and Apollyon encounters
Before a secondary phase inhabits my mind's
Midway application for maybe there will be
No secondary phase at all.

I remember a bronze girl stilled to burning sculpture
At a seaside place in summer time
And she was much more evident than others
A full and proper long-legged shape
For whom surrender meant marriage at the very least.
A damsel born not for dire distress,
Her penultimate, a fortnightly lodge
At Ballybunion, Youghal or Kilkee.

For winter to show her respectability
A beaver short-coat, Canadian squirrel three-quarter
And of course one full-length reputable musquash
And all through spring, autumn, summer, winter
An income from sedate and settled husband
Who will not spend a long weekend in London;
A limited number of children, all paragons.

I might have, if it were worth the time,
Apprenticed her to my way of thinking,
Shown her the imperturbability of dead leaves
In wordless woods of late autumn
Or stilled her lips with kisses if she chattered
When larks rose carolling from deep heather.

Then there was another maid of several sorts,
A creature whose eyes were luminous with love
Of places and people but notably herself
Who could not hear my loving undertones
For chance of not being seen at gatherings mostly
    theatrical.
Love's great passionate function was lost
Within her tedious tirades;
She could not stand Algernon Fitzpelligory.
You will have guessed he was an actor,
And that bitch Gillian Goodbody who played principal
Last year in *Puss and Boots* at Brighton,
And Dottie Dollydill, spiteful little wretch
Always ogling Otty Pussboy the impresario.
You would hardly expect a man of developing principle
To endure an endlessness of this.

I smote unplaned and springing boards in Morna
To wild accordeon and fiddle music.
I seized a red-legged thumper of a mountain lass
And waltzed her into breathlessness.
She suspected my thin towny accent from the start.
I eluded her kinsmen and fled that strange country.

It is a far cry from Morna of the brown bogs
To Paris of the gowns and green eye-shadow.
Now a decade later there is nothing so remote

As that erotic ambuscade upon femininity.
I sought the dark-haired white-faced girl
That I mentioned in an earlier chapter
And still dream that a shadowed street-corner
Or puce-lipped ponce of Paris might have located her.

Ah, pale girl of my dreams, you have entangled my
    loving,
Beset me with utter hopelessness.
In loneliness of sibilant midnight alleyways in Dublin
I have heard as far away as daybreak
Your tinkling thrilling laughter
But saw only the moon's light upon the grey slates of
    houses.
I knew, without you, the dread and searing loneliness
Of moonlit shadows without companionship.

Oh, pale girl of my dreams, I call out to you shamelessly.
Do not mistrust me for I shall fondle
The white toes of your feet without ceasing
From the hour of the loping wolves of dawn
Til the time of the loving-couples of evening.

Ah, pale girl of my dreams, my sanctuary,
Forever now you have me searching the sunlit glades
And secret places along the river of my birthplace.
I am addled and sore with muted, sad desire
To count, kindergarten-wise, the ten fingers of your hands.

Oh, pale girl of my heart, you have me at my wit's end
For never shall I feel under my fingers
The moist short-cropped hair of your head
Nor fondle the petals of your limp endearing ears
Or watch your white feet in a pool of clear water.

Oh, lost girl of my dreams, you have bewitched me.
I crave the dun, dark buds of your breasts
The whispering-out of our lying in deepest of darkness.

A Madman

I do not like the way
He wears his clothes
Yet I abide him.
And how I loathe the way
Another grows
Upon a new identity
And bawls all rights denied him.
I call them friends
And to what ends?
You say, seek hermitage!
I can't confront myself.
Man, that's the end of all.

I do not like
The fashion after which
A certain fellow blows
About some rich
Uncultured relative he knows,
Nor can I stand
The grand and pompous cry
Of sanctity,
That foul and shrieking lie
For I know very well
That if Christ walked again
The sanctified priest's bell
Would toll for his unmentionable hell.
And as for abstract things
Like song and love and verse
I will be terse

And say that these are part
Of an uncanny scheme,
A set of toys.

Then should I stand aside awhile
And let things pass me by!
And having learned
How to talk about the moil
Stand out and shout aloud.
I would, of course, be maimed,
Or else proclaimed
A madman, by the crowd.

To Charles Lynch

Fingers assembled hovering
Then the subtle chord
The muted delicacy.
I sit in the warm glow
Of peach-tinted melody,
Of bringing to mind
The labyrinthine cloisters
Of time and love and truth,
The sweet impossible recapture
Of purity and youth.
Enthroned he sits,
King of multitudinous cadences.
Eternally the rapture
Of loving splendour lingers.
I admire a most glorious soul.
I salute irreproachable fingers.

Charles Lynch [1906–1984] well known pianist

Words Taken from the
Latter Chapters of a Booze

We drank whiskey. We drank wine,
Myself and other self divine
And I found out I really was
Another entity, a clause
Of some unbodied second one.

I rose up quickly from my chair
And found that someone else was there,
Someone where I should have been,
Someone who is never seen,
Who was before I was begun.

In sodden haste I sat again
And tried to find out where and when
I found myself, my godly state
With hunger I put on a plate
Some small sardines and quickly ate.

I rose up sensibly enough
Was fully drunk and in a huff
Addressed this fellow, said: 'My liege
I'll thank you for my lost prestige.'
Needless to say no answer came.

I mentioned who I was. I said
I won some property, a bed
Where lovely partner waits, and she
Thinks more than all the world of me.

By this time I had guessed his game.
I pleaded pity, madness too,
And when that failed I called a crew
Of phantom allies round me to
Destroy this adamantine Jew
But could not lift my hand to kill.

I think he outmanoeuvred us,
Because he said, who wants a fuss.
Besides I've helped you more than I
Should really. If you want to die
Do so, but I say drink your fill.

To a Girl of Eighteen in a Cocktail Lounge which is Filled with Old Women

She sat near purple draperies
On high stool 'throned, her velvet knees
And silken throat and breasts concealed
But barely with foothills revealed
Were magnets of attention there
Where most are too polite to stare
But every covert glance stole she
She knew she was delight to see
She delicately stroked her coif
And thighs as well defined as if
The garments glued to bulbous flesh
Were far away as Marrakesh
While fatted folk of selfsame sex
She scoffed at and for sure did vex
And showed no trace of shame or fear.
It was her time, her place, her year.

Come Destiny

Come destiny and sup with us and hope and fate
Tell why you abide us, for what better dreaming.
Drink deeply. Tell us why the latticed gate
Closes the garden where bright light is gleaming.

Come tell us of remembrance and the dead host that brings
The sound of music and each dawn that blows
The flame of passion on tomorrow's wings
Whither all joy and sorrow and the puny mortal goes.

For we are tired of meanings, dimmed by placid phrases,
Wearied of all music and all philosophic mazes.
Jargons of the tongues have fooled us with expression
And beauty ever-pleasing has but kept us in procession.

Home

I

Something has burned up my heart.
Something of youth and years and places,
Old spreading trees, noise of a passing cart,
Small romping boys and care on people's faces,
Wan, weary women trudging up and down,
Tall, blue mountains rising far away,
Sad, endless thoughts of my home town,
And dreams to fill the long empty day.

II

An old hound crying in the night,
Soft loveliness of leaves and rushing waters
Waking a boy again, confused with fright.
My father's voice; the stir of nature's daughters
I feel the soft rain in my face.
I hear the fireside tales, the love, the laughter
Echoing low in this far distant place
Leaving me to mourn alone the long hours after.

Faces

There are faces I remember
From June days long ago,
Faces of cold November,
Old men I used to know.
And memory embraces
Faces of March and May,
From half-remembered places –
Faces of yesterday.

Dear faces I have cherished;
Suckling shapes of youth,
Cherub and love long perished,
Hers of stony truth.
Sad innocents unsullied,
Gentle, cleft of chin,
And faces I have bullied
With sleight of mind to sin.

Leaving Home for the First Time

Oh, my love, my first love, lie down here beside me.
Oh, my love, my dear love, oh, sweet love, betide me.
Lie still in my arms; do not moan, love, or tremble:
The wild doves are sleeping high on the green bramble.

All over Feale river the shadows are falling.
And deep in Shanowen the vixen is calling.
The sweet night is young, love; the night is forever.
And shadows are falling all over Feale river.

I would fly like a bird with white wings in the air,
Or swim the wild waters far off into Clare.
Come close, love. Come closer. Look deep in the pool, love.
Was ever love-making so tender or true, love?

Oh, my love, my first love, the salmon are leaping.
Lie still, my hard heart, my beloved is sleeping.
The sweet night is young, love; tonight is forever.
The shadows are falling all over Feale river.

Honour

I would love to be combing her hair,
To lay the strands over my hands.
I would spy with the stealth of a stoat
The pulse of her pandurate wrist,
And admire the sweet shape of her throat
And the grand and languinous lands
Of her legs and her ankles and twist
The necks of the feckless that dare
To dishonour her name when she's missed.

My Father

When he spoke gustily and sincerely
Spittle fastened
Not merely upon close lapel
But nearly blinded
Those who had not hastened
To remove pell-mell.
He was inviolate.
Clung to old stoic principle,
And he
Dismissed his weaknesses
As folly.
His sinning was inchoate;
Drank ill-advisedly.
His waistcoat I remember –
Tobacco-perfumed parallelogram
Of pennied pockets.
Once when unexpected telegram
Advised immediate payment
Eyes rocketed in sockets
At demand of claimant.
He wired this cant:
'Coffers rent apart.
Am intimate friend
Of Weller, Tony.
Have ripped beadles apart.
Am, sir, compelled to dial
The number of your heart.'
I am terribly proud of my father,
Bitterly, faithfully proud.

Let none say a word to my father
Or mention his name out loud.
I adored his munificent blather
Since I was his catch-as-catch-can.
I am terribly proud of my father
For he was a loveable man.

John B. was deeply attached to his father, William Keane, and spoke lovingly about him up to his own demise in May 2002. Headmaster at Clounmacon National School, William Keane would cycle or walk to the school, which was situated three miles from the town of Listowel. He passed away on 8 August 1963 at the age of 73.

The Tumbler of Men

I remember a house on a hill
And a bocketty mountain man
And a labouring man with his fill
Of work since his days began.

These incidents happened in Lyre
When I was a child of eight,
The labouring man in the byre,
The other man strung on a gate.

They directed invective at me
But I had grown used to the game.
Freely and gladly, with glee,
I cursed them, without any shame.

The good priest back in the glen
Condemned them. He justly felt
They were particular devils, these men,
Who loved the black draught of the Celt.

I met the priest from the glen
No more than a season ago.
He poured me the tumbler of men
And told me the story so.

The old man won't feel it so much
For he was well used to the fire;
But the labourer will, he was such
As was used to the cold of the byre.

Ballad of Survival

We called every man 'sir!'
Who wore collar and tie.
We died when our betters died,
Old woman, you and I.

In the town they laughed at me
And they called you a plaster.
We hid from the sight of the priest
And ran a mile from the Master.

In drink I was wild and coarse.
Lout with a filthy mouth.
The guards assisted the rich
And assisted me with a clout.

But we made the finest of men
No different from the rest.
And girls as pure as a spring,
The identical same as the best.

And we courted under a rick
In the mild and the wild of weathers
And we loved on a downy tick
Of green goose feathers.

We'll call every man 'Sir!'
Who wears collar and tie.
We'll die when our betters die,
Old woman, you and I.

Women who Idolise Dogs

I will not have a dog for a pet
Nor a sleek, smug cat.
I might regard them as friends
And leave it at that.

No, I would even prefer
A fat dissoluble tart.
I would lavish attention on her
And love of a human heart.

Or, in a bibulous mood,
I might set eyes on a child
Lost in a penniless brood
Of twenty or more and unspoiled;

Spin him a long line of bunk,
Put a five-pound note in his hand:
Intimate I was his unc'.
Depart with the swish of a wand.

But women with dogs I abhor,
The selfish unfeminine bitches.
There are good men who need you much more
And children who think you are witches.

A Young Father's Advice to his Sons

They say to walk away is quite correct.
Ignore the brawl and fast by-pass the frown.
But what if men are kicked when they are down –
Jew, Catholic, black men, white men or brown?

Never walk away, my beloved few.
Turn the deaf ear to the canting crew.
Christ was crucified. Where was faithful friend
To ambush the unwilling
Mercenaries who wrought His end?

The Drinkers

Our anthem is the dismal whine
Of every swinging sighing sign
That sobs the nakedness of night.
Our foe, the bitter icy wind
That snaps upon us from behind.
Our battle-plain the gutter.
Hear the harsh drum splutter!
Was it peering woman's finger
Drawing her venetian blind?
Not for us the deep draught
Of bull-neckedness, oh, no!
Neither lusts nor anger,
Mighty passion's glow.
Woman is not ours to claim.
We know she has one other name;
She is beauty, beauty, beauty,
Not a conquerable foe.
Our end to bury beauty
With a darkness that is duty
And to drive the leaden anguish from the mind,
From the drear, sere mind.

Other Men's Sons

I am not one of those,
Nor friends of their sons.
I am suspect. Let it be so.
I gather they will be slow to consider
My contribution.
I will not be of anyone.
Nor would he have it thus
Nor shall I, continuing his principle,
Shower favours at my disposal
Upon mine, at risk of wounding
Other men's sons.

Crinny Hill

I left Crinny Hill
Before the light of day.
I kissed and loved my fill
And gave my love away.

It was neither day nor dawn
Upon the mountain's rim,
But the time of lost and gone
And the time of dead and dim.

I sat upon a stone.
I listened long and well.
I sat still and alone
And here is what befell.

Wings of the Goureen Roe*
Stirring the faint frost,
Bleating high and low,
But what I felt is lost.

Dead and lost and gone
Finished for evermore
A charge from a fowler's gun,
A lisp in the sea's roar.

I might have understood
The mood of the brown bog,
The black cow at her cud,
The strange talk of the frog.

I might have kissed the lips
Of black night herself
And traced with my finger tips
The face of the dark elf;

Or tripped on the white trail
Of the river down the glen
And woven a wonderful tale
For the ears of the wise men.

Goureen Roe, i.e., Jacksnipe.

Two Lips

Two lips whose sweetness and delight
Is gentle like the summer night,
Whose lingering breath and whisper seems
More musical than silver streams,
Whose moist impression is more fair
Than dewfall in the moonlight air.

Two lips whose beauty and whose fire
Have taught me all my heart's desire,
Whose kiss is with me night and day,
Whose every prayer I must obey.

Two lips whose tender grace is such
They tremble at my finger's touch,
Whose velvet loveliness imparts
The sweetness in her heart of hearts.

John B. met Mary O'Connor of Ahaneboy, Knocknagoshel during the
Listowel Races in 1949 at a dance in Walshe's ballroom. They married
in Knocknagoshel church on 5 January 1955. This is one of the many
poems he wrote in celebration of her.

Two Eyes

Two eyes that beam with early dawn,
Two eyes that sleep when night comes on.

Two eyes that gently break on me
As little waves out of the sea,
Over a drear and dismal shore
With silver feet and joy once more.

Two eyes that teach me how to live.
How to receive and how to give.

How to acknowledge and to bless,
How to accept defeat and shame.

How from descending to ascend
How to come nearer to my end.

Two eyes where I shall find always
Repose from weary nights and days.

Two eyes whose beauty in my heart,
I feel when we are far apart,

Where should the tiniest tear awake,
I know my very soul should break,
And all things other cease to be.
Those two eyes mean so much to me.

First published in The Kerryman, *March 1950.*

Autumn's End

With upturned bellies lying cold
In habits black and striped with gold
Behind large windows of glass plate
Dead, swollen wasps accumulate.
Small monkeys in their northern zoos
Grumble with unaccustomed 'flu's'.
Fat frogs harrumph and blurp in peace
On harvest bellies white as fleece
And in the wells the water's free
From beetle, bug and buzzing bee.
Soft salmon redden in the pools
And lazy squirrels shout: 'Down tools!'
Moist green leaves rest in rotting rust.
Hot donkeys roll no more in dust.

Delight

I

There is delight, and dear desire
Where no sadness lingers
There is such joy and gentle fire
In her pale, cool fingers.

II

Deep in her eyes there lies
Lovely beyond a name,
Blue-mist of moon-filled skies
That blows my heart to flame.

III

Calm is her voice and sweet
As laughter of fairest songs;
To the soft tread of her feet
Each grace I know belongs.

IV

There is magic beyond decline
And moist as the rose dew-tips,
There is delight like olden wine
In her red, rare lips.

V

No poet or bard inspired
Could sing her praises true,
Even I who have found my lyre
In the mist of her eyes of blue.

VI

She is near me by day and night
And yet she is far away,
The dawning of my delight,
The sun of my early day.

Written on 14 February 1950

Tryst

I

Tonight you promised you would come
And meet me by the hazel-wood,
With saddest thought my heart is numb,
Because I thought you understood,
And now the voice of spring is dumb,
There is no laughter in the flood.

II

There is no music in the air,
No nightingale has come to sing,
No love, no laughter anywhere,
I am alone with all the spring,
The starry sky that once was fair,
Is now a blighted bleary thing.

III

And were you laughing all the time,
When you were wafting with my dreams,
The wan white moon is out of rhyme,
For you have mocked my heart it seems,
And to a more enchanted clime,
Belong these little silver streams.

IV

Joy! It is you behind the bough,
I thought you had forgotten this,
I could have wept my love, but now
My every tear will be of bliss.

The spring is fair and pure I vow,
But not so sweet as my love's kiss.

Written on 28 February 1950

Yesterday

I

Close by the river sang the bird,
Do you remember how we heard
Sweet music that was wild and gay
Among the brambles yesterday?

II

Do you remember how our hearts
Were filling with such sweet delight,
Not thinking, soon how we must part
My poor oul' Mague and I that night?

III

Do you remember how your hair
Was tossed, and how your eyes were blue?
I will remember everywhere,
And every time I think of you.

IV

My sweet one always fills my heart,
More than my songs or words can say,
But Mary, my life's loveliest part
Was by the river yesterday.

Written on 14 May 1951

Dan Paddy Andy

As I went out through the land of Lyre
The beaded dews did the fields attire
And the old, grey world was turned to fire
In the month of May in the morning
Out of the bowers by the bright sun lit,
Lark and linnet and long-tailed tit
And every other that ever did flit
Sang loud of the sun's adorning

Sand from the foliage green and gay,
Sang from the love of the newborn day
Sang for the blossoming buds of May
And sang for the rude and the randy
Sang for a soul unsung, unloved,
Sang for a spirit too long reproved
As over the Ivy Bridge I roved
To the land of Dan Paddy Andy.

And there stood Dan with a pipe in his hand
Saying 'come away now to the promised land
For I know a dame wants a ring for her hand
And for bells in her ears to be ringing'.
Oh blessed the land that shimmering hour
Blossoms bursting on every bower
Hedgerows white with the thorn in flower
And the whole world sweetly singing.

And there in the sycamore's misty shade
there waited a bountiful, beautiful maid

A mystical, madrigal, marrying maid
The shadows and dark shades scorning
And as the blazing sun climbed higher,
They roved through the blossoming land of Lyre
And the songbirds sang in colossal choir
When he kissed his love in the morning.

*Lines written at the Ivy Bridge, Renagowen, Lyreacrompane to com-
memorate Dan Paddy Andy O'Sullivan [1899–1966], last of the great
matchmakers, 18 May 1982.*

*John B. was greatly impressed by this amiable character who suc-
cessfully matched several couples in his lifetime.*

The Gallant Greenville Team

Come all ye true-born Irishmen
From here to Healy's Gate,
And I'll sing for you a verse or two
As I my tale relate.
You may speak about Cuchulainn bold
Or the mighty men from Sneem,
But they wouldn't hold a candle
To that Greenville team.

'Ha-Ha!' said Billeen Sweeney,
'Sure I'll tackle up my ass
And I'll put on my brown suit
That I wear goin' to mass.
I'll hit the road to Listowel town
By the morning's airy beam,
And I'll bring home Berkie's mutton
For that gallant Greenville team!'

'The dry ball won't suit 'em',
Said the pundits from the town,
But they pulverised the Ashes,
And they mesmerised the Gleann.
Next came the famous Boro,
Their fortunes to redeem,
But they shrivelled up the autumn leaves
Before the Greenville team.

''Twas the white trout that done the trick'
John L. was heard to say,

'We ate 'em mornin' noon and night
In the run-up to the fray.
They hardened up the muscles
And they built up the steam,
Until no power on earth could beat
The gallant Greenville team.'

Written in 1961 as a tribute to the Greenville team for their prowess on the football field during the local Town Leagues. Greenville is a leafy suburb on the outskirts of Listowel; Berkie Brown was a local butcher.

The Brown Hills of Meen

When I hear the sweet music of streams at my feet
And the lack of his paradise carolling sweet,
I remember the brown hills and valleys so green.
And the soft purple heather that blossoms in Meen.

Then my heart journeys back to the joys once I knew.
I recall in my dreaming two sweet eyes of blue,
And with sadness I think of the sights I have seen
And the dear folk I loved on the brown hills of Meen.

Let your valley men sing of their meadows of gold,
Of their lakes that are silver and a joy to behold.
But for me there is sweeter than silver or sheen.
In the brown hills and heather that blossoms in Meen.

Like the laugh of a boy is the wind there that blows.
Like the cheek of a maiden, the wild mountain rose.
And the brook at Deangcuman through channels unseen,
Sings welcome and murmurs the beauty on Meen.

And if ever a fortune of gold I amass,
Through your cities and townships of fame I will pass,
And a small cottage built where the wild curlews keen.
Near the people I love on the brown hills of Meen.

So farewell to the heather and hearts that are true.
I am going alas from the brown hills and you.
With sadness I leave for a strange foreign scene.
Far away from the heather and the brown hills of Meen.

The Sive Song

To be sung

Oh, come all good men and true, a sad tale I'll tell to you
Of the maiden who was known to me as Sive.
She was young and sweet and fair but that household sad
    and bare
Her marriage to an old man would contrive.

To be recited

Now the Tinker's son came in to that house of want and sin
And his father Pats Bocock smote on the floor
Saying 'Carthalawn, my blade, let a noble song be made
Bringing plenty on this house for evermore.'

To be sung

Oh Mike Glavin, you're the man; you was always in the
    van
With an open door to oul' man and gorsoon
May white snuff be at your wake, bakers bread and
    curran-y cake
And the plenty on your table late and soon.

To be recited

But they scorned the Tinker's son when his song of praise
    was done
And his father Pats Bocock smote on the floor

Saying 'Carthalawn my jewel, let a song both wild and cruel
Settle down upon this house for evermore'.

To be sung

On the road from Abbeyfeale, sure I met a man with meal
Come here says he and pass your idle time;
On me he made quite bold, saying the young will wed the
     old
And the old man have the money for the child.

To be recited

Now Thomasheen Rua the liar, was sat down 'longside the
     fire
And he sold the girl Sive that very night
Pats Bocock made on his quest, saying 'sing your mighty
     best'.
And the song of Carthalawn was like a blight.

To be sung

May the snails devour his corpse, and the rains do harm
     worse,
May the devil sweep the hairy creature soon,
He's as greedy as a sow, as a crow behind the plough
The black man from the mountain, Seánín Rua.

May he screech with awful thirst, may his brains and eye-
     balls burst,
That melted amadán, that big bostoon.
May the fleas ate up his bed, and the mange consume his
     head
The black man from the mountain, Seánín Rua.

To be recited

But the Bonny Sive took flight, like a wild bird in the night
And the waters washed her small white body o'er
And her true love found her there, and he stacked her golden hair
And he laid her on the dark and dismal shore.

Then outspoke bold Pats Bocock and his voice was sad with shock
And his face was grey as winter when he cried.
He said 'Carthalawn, my gem, let you make a woeful hymn
All of this day and of the one who died.'

To be sung

Oh, come all good men and true, a sad tale I'll tell to you
All of a maiden fair who died this day.
Oh, they drownded lovely Sive, for she would not be a bride
And they laid her dead to bury in the clay.

Sweet Listowel

Oh sweet Listowel I've loved you all my days.
Your towering spires and shining streets and squares
Where sings the Feale its overlasting lays
And whispers to you in its evening prayers

Chorus

Of all fair towns few have so sweet a soul
Or gentle folk compassionate and true.
Where'er I go I'll love you sweet Listowel
And doff my distant cap each day to you.

Down by the Feale the willows dip their wands
From magic bowers where soft the night wind sighs.
How oft I've roved along your moonlit lands
Where late love blooms and first love never dies.

Chorus

Of all fair towns few have so sweet a soul
Or gentle folk compassionate and true.
Where'er I go I'll love you sweet Listowel
And doff my distant cap each day to you.

Written as promised to Eric Browne, neighbour and bookie.

Bunagara by the Feale

There's an emerald bright in Ireland's fair tiara.
It's just a mile or two outside Listowel.
'Tis a pleasant spot. They call it Bunagara
Sure 'twould steal away the teardrops from your soul.

Chorus

Take me back again to dear old Bunagara
To that spot beloved of salmon, trout and eel,
Far away from all the noise and tatarara
On the banks of Bunagara by the Feale.

You may search from Timbuctoo to Toomevara.
You may travel from Kanturk to Botany Bay,
But you'll never find the likes of Bunagara
On the banks of Bunagara by the Feale.

Chorus

And when the rifle fire came down the mountain,
Our heroes fought like badgers in their gore.
The blood it flowed like water from a fountain
On the banks of Bunagara long ago.

Chorus

There the cat and dog are faster than the norm
And this is known by sportsmen near and far,
Sure the Kingdom Cup it never saw such form
When that cup was won by Crafty Shalimar.

Chorus

Invocation

I sing of Tubberduff and Tubberbawn
Lest in the distant future a day dawn
When o'er their deeds forgetfulness is drawn
And therefore I beseech you Holy Ghost
Fly to my aid with all your heavenly host
So that those glorious teams I now may toast.
And so I kneel upon the old green grass
Where men aspire to fame that does not pass
I raise my hands and lift aloft my glass
As I salute those souls who fielded high
And plucked the pigskin from the bluebell sky
And soloed sweetly when the sun was high.

Sonnet

You'll never corner me inside
Nor catch me on the wide outside
For I who thrive by dint of the pen
Am never without and never within.

But am where the rough and ready lout
May never be heard though loud his shout
May never look in while I look out.

And there neither bias nor exposé
May sully the sun, distort my day
Or ravish my night till it's fretted away.

So all who would cherish a sacred muse
Must sanely, soberly, solemnly choose
Neither the outside nor the in
But the gossamer line that lies between.

Written in May 1987

The Alder Tree

Today I walked to meet my alder
The alder I had loved for fourteen years
The brown bog's finest feature
How I loved its autumn's russet
Its winter's filigree
Its budded spring
Its flickering silvery green
In breezy summer days.
But when I came
My alder tree was dead
Maimed and stripped
By schoolboys heedless
Contrite when confronted
We never knew,
Nobody told us they said
That alders mattered.

Written in May 1987

Many Young Men of Twenty

Many young men of twenty said goodbye
All that long day,
From break of dawn till the sun was high
Many young men of twenty said goodbye

My boy Jimmy, went that day
On the big ship sailed away
Sailed away and left me here to die
Many young men of twenty said goodbye

My Jimmy said he'd sail across the sea
He swore his oath
He'd sail again, back home to marry me
My Jimmy said he'd sail across the sea
But my Jimmy left me down
O, my Jimmy, please come back to me!
O, my Jimmy, please come back to me!

Many young men of twenty said goodbye
It breaks my heart, to see the face of girl and boy
It breaks my heart and now I'm fit to die

My boy Jimmy's, gone from me
Sailed away across the sea
Jimmy's gone and here alone am I
Many young men of twenty said goodbye

Many young men of twenty said goodbye
All that long day,

From break of dawn till the sun was high
Many young men of twenty said goodbye

They left the mountain and the glen
The lassies and the fine young men
I saw the tears of every girl and boy

Many young men of twenty said goodbye
Many young men of twenty said goodbye.

As Simple as ABC

Let X be equal to my love for you
It's as simple as ABC
Because I'm a mathematician in the very best tradition
So let X be equal to my love for you.
Let Y be equal to your love for me
It's as simple as ABC
Put the X and the Y together and we'll soon discover
    whether
We will mingle mathematically.
Take the square root of love and divide by the stars above
Take one quarter of a moon and a sweet romantic tune
Take a circle from a ring you're sure to see mathematically.
Let Y be equal to your love for me
It's as simple as ABC
Put the X and the Y together and we'll soon discover
    whether
We will mingle mathematically
It's as simple as ABC.

From Many Young Men of Twenty

The Boot Factory

I haven't got a million but I'm going to settle down
This morning I decided for to rent a place in town
I wrote my love a letter saying will you marry me?
I've lately got employment in the boot factory.

In the boot factory, in the boot factory
I've lately got employment in the boot factory.

I haven't got a million but it doesn't worry me
It doesn't cost a million for to marry in Tralee.
Soon she'll have my letter and she'll come along with me
Because I've got employment in the boot factory.

In the boot factory, in the boot factory
Because he's got employment in the boot factory.

Chorus:
I haven't got a million but I'm going to settle down
This morning I decided for to rent a place in town
I wrote my love a letter saying will you marry me?
I've lately got employment in the boot factory.

In the boot factory, in the boot factory
I've lately got employment in the boot factory.

From Roses of Tralee

Won't You Come Under my Shawl?

Won't you come under my shawl,
When my heart is as light as a feather?
Why don't you answer my call
When my eyes advertise a come hither?

Won't you come under my shawl?
Sure my shawl is the best place of all
And it's nice to be there, when there's frost in the air.
Please won't you come under my shawl?

I'll never know what I've missed
But I tried with my greatest endeavour.
By others I've often been kissed
Since the day that you left me forever.

Won't you come under my shawl?
I have loved you the best of them all.
But you had your pride and you went from my side
Far away from the folds of my shawl.

Won't you come under my shawl,
When my heart is as light as a feather?
Why don't you answer my call,
When my eyes advertise a come hither?

Won't you come under my shawl?
Sure my shawl is the best place of all
And it's nice to be there, when there's frost in the air,
Please won't you come under my shawl?

Camden Town

Kind folks, you'll beg my pardon
I'm far from my country,
For Camden town's my garden
And the Thames my nursery.

I hear the boughbells ringing
And the song they sing for me
Is the merry song of Camden
Where I long to be.

I'm far away from home
From tall building and blue dome
If I were back, I'd never roam
From Camden town, my home.

Let all the world go crazy
What's it got to do with me?
I must go back to Camden
Where I long to be.

I'm far away from home
From tall building and blue dome
If I were back, I'd never roam
From Camden town, my home.

From Roses of Tralee

The Servant Girl

I am a servant girl, fair game to one and all
At thirty bob a week, I am the beck and call
The Golf Club won't have me as you can plainly see
I am the servant girl, the Miss in Misery.

All this is very fine, the drinking and the song;
It happens all the time, why must it happen wrong?
How simple now for you to say that you'll be true?
How simple now for me to whisper – I love you!

But when the dance is done, no star will shine on me
I'll be a servant girl, and you'll be fancy free
No handsome prince I meet, with slipper for my feet
I am the servant girl, the Miss in Misery.

From Many Young Men of Twenty

Off to Tralee

We're off to Tralee, Uncle Jimmy and me.
He's the right age to see I'm the rage in high society.
We're off to Tralee, cold out here, imagine you're an icicle
Change down gears, please remember you're free.
You see more of the country on a bicycle,
Hurryin', worryin' people worry me.

We're off to Tralee, Uncle Jimmy and me.
He has the means, I have the teens and popularity.
We're off to Tralee, I don't care
What's the point in hurrying?
I don't care, specially since the country is free.
I don't care, what's the point in worryin'?
Hurryin', worryin' people worry me.
We're off to Tralee, we're off to Tralee, we're off to Tralee.

From Roses of Tralee

Let the Dance Go On

Let the dance go on young people everywhere
Arise and shine appear as fresh as dew.
Let the dance go on and let each happy pair
Whisper the words, my darling I love you.

Love you alone and no one else my dear
This is the theme that makes the world go around
For distant stars I know I'll never care
All that I crave is having you around.

Let the dance go on young people everywhere
Arise and shine appear as fresh as dew.
Let the dance go on and let each happy pair
Whisper the words, my darling I love you.

Keelty

Oh my love, my lost one, soon the roses must die
And soon the wild duck will fly hard on the sky.
Oh my love, my lost one, do not leave me to die
For the strength and love of you, down here in Keelty.

I'll be waiting for you, where the cockerel cries
Down here in Keelty, where the heart in me dies.
I'll be waiting for you, where the heart in me sighs
For the strength and love of you, down here in Keelty.

I'll be waiting for you, where the small waters flow
Down here in Keelty, where the whitethorn grow
The white fires of joy in your bosom will glow
When you see your fine young son, down here in Keelty.

From Many Young Men of Twenty

If I Were the Rose of Tralee

If I were the Rose of Tralee
What a wonderful night it would be.
I would walk like a queen
I would talk like a queen
But I know that it never can be.
I'm just a plain Jane, but I'm hoping in vain
That they'll see something special in me.

I've been hated and stared at by all
To see if I'm too short or too tall.
I've patiently stood for as long as I could
And now I'm so tired I could fall.
But I'll stand here all night
In the hope that I might
Be selected as belle of the ball.

If I were the Rose of Tralee
But I haven't a chance as you see.
Still all is not lost and my fingers are crossed
But it just couldn't happen to me.
I'm poised on a ledge and my nerves are on edge
And I'm tossed like a cork on the sea
Cork on the sea, cork on the sea.

If I were the Rose of Tralee
What a wonderful night it would be.
I would walk like a queen
I would talk like a queen
But I know that it never can be.

I'm just a plain Jane, but I'm hoping in vain
That they'll see something special in me.

From Roses of Tralee

The Buck Navvy Song

Come all ye true born Irish men, and listen to my song,
I am a bold buck navvy and I don't know right from wrong.
Of late I was transported boys, from Éireann's holy shore,
My case is sad, my crime is bad, for I was born poor.

And if you're born poor me boys, that is a woeful state
The judge will sit upon your crime and this he will relate,
'I find the prisoner guilty, and the law I must lay down,
Let this man be transported straight away to Camden town.'

'Then take him down to Cricklewood and lock him in the
    pub
And call the limey governor and propose him for the sub.
Yes, take him down to Cricklewood, to mortar, bricks and
    lime,
And let him rot in Cricklewood, until he serves his time.'

Oh Cricklewood, oh Cricklewood, you stole my youth away,
For I was young and innocent, but you were old and grey.

*Buck navvies were the men who built the roads of England, who did the
dirty work of digging and pickaxing, of bending, of lifting, of smiting
and of shovelling. These were the men who built the power stations and
the oil refineries, the tunnels and the bridges.*

*John B. emigrated to England in 1951 in order to save enough
money to buy a business so that he could marry Mary O'Connor. He
would have met and worked with many a buck navvy there, until he
returned to Listowel in 1953.*

Kitty Curley

I love pretty, Kitty Curley,
'Deed I do, 'deed I do,
Love her late, I love her early
Love her cos her teeth are pearly
I love pretty Kitty Curley
'Deed I do, 'deed I do.

When I land in dear Dáil Éireann
Kitty, I will marry you.
An ermine coat you will be wearin'
The TDs' wives will all be tearin',
I love pretty Kitty Curley
'Deed I do, 'deed I do.

Cross my palm or you're a gonner
I know what life holds for you.
I tells fortunes for a tanner
Tell the truth upon me honour
All the lads know Kitty Curley
'Deed they do, 'deed they do.

I'd sooner join the foreign legion
What in hell am I to do?
I've no wife or son or daughter
I've a chance across the water.
I love pretty Kitty Curley
'Deed I do, 'deed I do.

From Many Young Men of Twenty

The Liffey Side

Please let me hear the seabird crying
And see the swans go down the tide.
Carry me back when you hear me sighing,
Carry me back to the Liffey side.
I grew up on the Liffey side,
I grew up on the Liffey side,
Where the water is deep and wide
And the bells ring out on the Liffey side.
Bells ring out on the Liffey side.

There is a place which calls me ever
There is a spot where I would reside,
Over the wall and up the river
Over the wall where the ships are tied.
I grew up on the Liffey side,
I grew up on the Liffey side,
Where the water is deep and wide
And the bells ring out on the Liffey side.
Bells ring out on the Liffey side.

A time will come it's the time for leaving
A time that will not be denied.
Lift me up when you hear me grieving
And lay me down by the Liffey side.
I grew up on the Liffey side,
I grew up on the Liffey side,
Where the water is deep and wide
And the bells ring out on the Liffey side.
Bells ring out on the Liffey side.

The Dawn is Breaking

The dawn is breaking now
Where hills are wet with dew.
And in my lonely heart
Are memories of you.
There is no other love for me
You will be mine through all eternity.

You will be mine while stars of night are shining
And we shall dream until we meet again,
The stars have fled and shades of night are pining,
The dawn won't break, my love, until we meet again.

As I stand here and dream and once again I hear
Your soft voice in the glade,
High soars the lark through skies of blue
My heart will break with memories of you.

You will be mine while stars of night are shining
And we shall dream until we meet again,
The stars have fled and shades of night are pining
The dawn won't break, my love, until we meet again.